THIS BOOK BELONG TO:

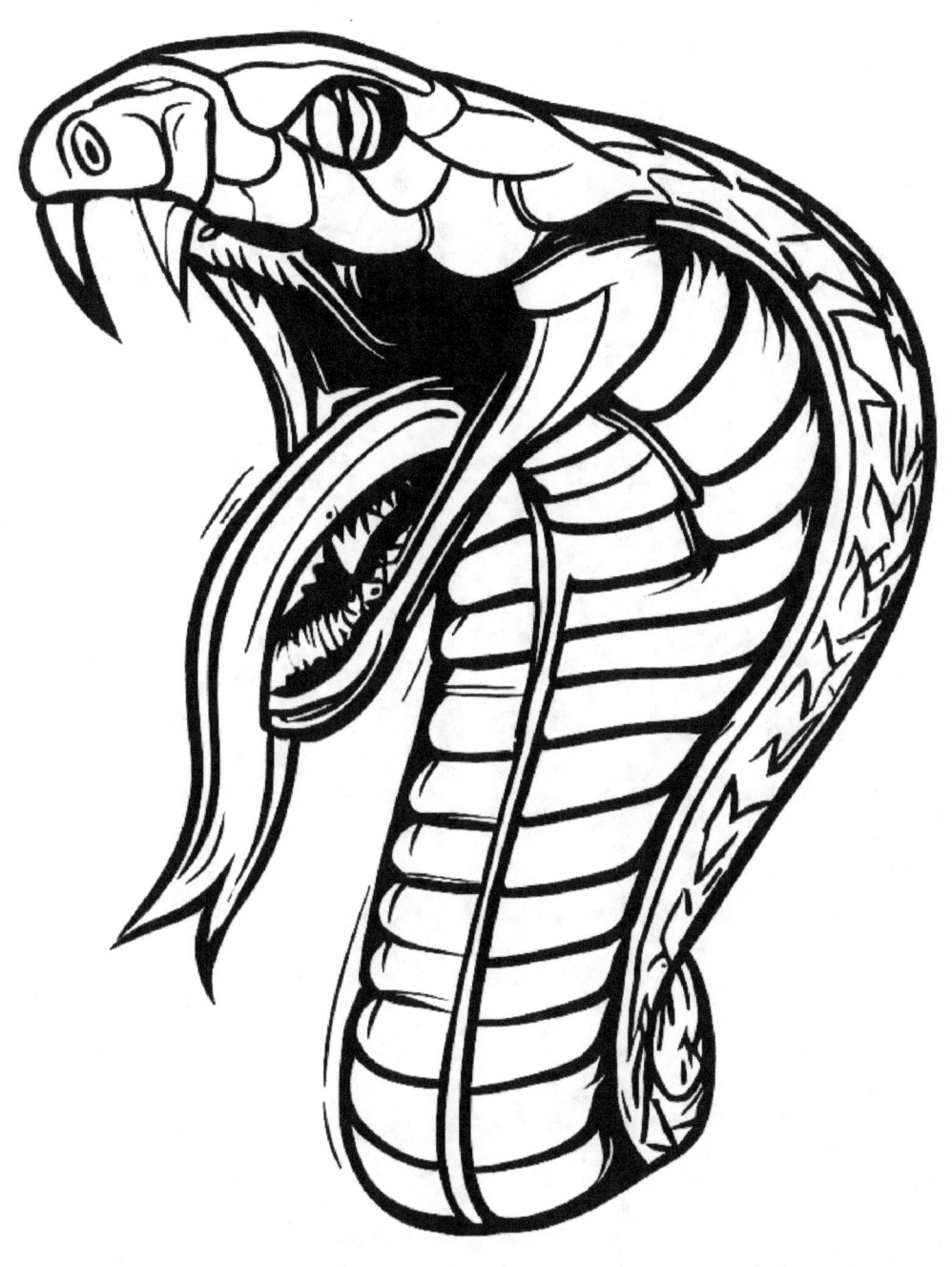

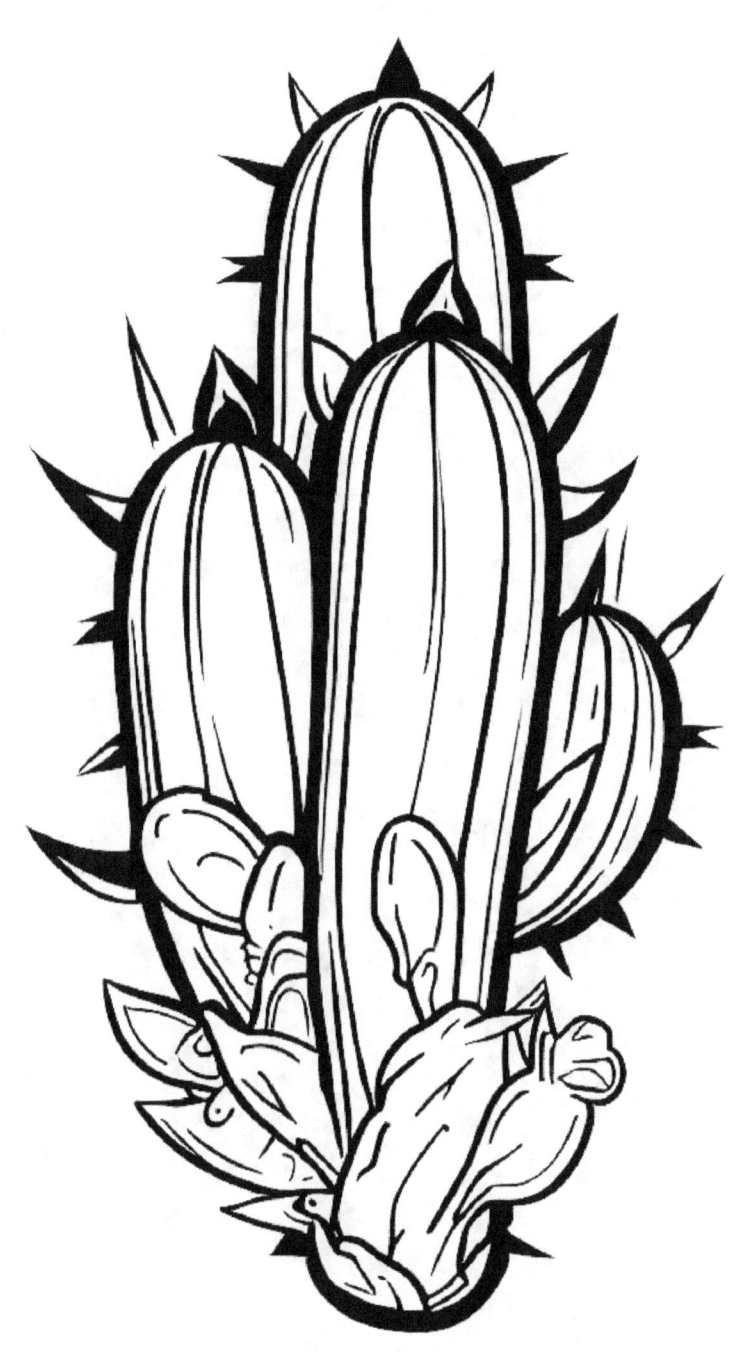

www.ingramcontent.com/pod-product-compliance
Lightning Source LLC
Chambersburg PA
CBHW081521220526
45467CB00010B/2997